Tiki Taka Passing Patterns & Exercises

Improving Players' Passing Speed & First Touch

By Marcus DiBernardo

Table of Contents

Tiki Taka Passing Patterns

Key Points and Objectives

Perhaps you are asking what exactly is a passing pattern and how will it make my team better? Passing patterns are designed patterns that players execute in a pre-set order. The patterns can range from very simple to very complex. The most important thing to remember when training passing patterns is that "the secret is in the details"—the firmness of the pass, proper timing and movement of the receiving player, proper body position of the player receiving the ball, proper technique of the passer and receiver, eye contact with receiver before passing the ball, using correct passing and receiving surface, establishing a rhythm of play with teammates, executing the drill at a challenging level and always remaining focused.

I remember watching the Technical Director of Liverpool FC giving a training session. He started out the session with the "Star" Passing Pattern used at FC Barcelona. The major coaching point in this exercise and all his exercises was "the details matter". If the players did not focus on the details, the efficiency of the passing went down, meaning, play was slower. He went on to explain, that saving a split second, can be the difference between losing possession or not. If the player was not positioned correctly to receive the ball it might take an extra half a second to move the ball out from his feet. That extra half a second matters in ball circulation and retention. FC Barcelona is good because they save seconds all over the field. Allowing them to get rid of the ball before the other team can even pressure.

When coaching passing patterns the details are what make the training useful. Receiving players should come off their cone when the passing player receives the ball and their head is coming up (eye contact before passing the ball is required). If the two players work together like this; the result will produce coordinated movement that is realistic to a game situation. Movement at the right time is the key to creating separation. Move too early and you will have to wait for the ball giving the defender the chance to react. Move at the right time in coordination with the incoming pass and the defender has no chance. However, the weight of the pass must be game realistic. Firm passing to the <u>correct foot</u> is needed make the pattern realistic. Passing the ball firmly to the correct foot combined with proper timed movement will create a rhythm to the pattern. Once the pattern is running smoothly you will be able to pick up on the rhythm when observing. Patterns should also have a desired receiving and passing body part designated. Many of the Tiki Taka patterns require inside of foot passing. Getting the ball accurately moving around 1-touch at a fast paced tempo is the goal.

I personally believe passing patterns are directly applicable to the actual 11v11 game. Players can easily translate the passing movements, visual cues, timing and rhythm directly onto the pitch if the patterns are done in a realistic way. A fun way to make a pattern more game like is to add mental pressure. Have the groups doing the patterns race against each other. This will make every touch count and the speed of play will matter as well. The first team to complete the pattern 10 times is the winner. Watch to see how much more focused the players will become. Another option is to have players count the number of inaccurate passes they made during a three-minute period. They can reflect on their performance and try and cut down on the inaccurate passes for the next timed round. Using performance goals or objectives in training can be extremely effective. If a group did a passing pattern ten times successfully in three minutes write it down. Two weeks later the performance objective may be to do the same pattern eleven times in that same three-minute time frame.

I want to stress the point that in order for your players to improve they must be involved with "deliberate practice". Deliberate practice is basically very focused practice with the feedback of an experienced coach. It is important to teach the details, give players specific technical feedback, allow players to reflect on their performance, push players to play at the edge of their ability, make training competitive and have them understand that hard focused training is needed to improve.

I heard a good story about getting better & improving skill levels the other day. As expected, most people can drive a car every day and manage just fine. They attain a certain level of driving skill and stay at that level forever. However, the reality is most people do not gain any special driving skills after the first initial 50 hours of driving experience. This made me think that even though a person may be doing something 20 hours a week they may not be getting better at it. That is my point with passing patterns and all soccer training—practice needs to be deliberate and focused for players to consistently improve.

In order to get the most out of the passing patterns in this book focus on the "details", performance objectives and key points. If you do one passing pattern per day for 15 minutes, I guarantee you will see improvement in your player's ability to pass the ball and keep possession. Enjoy the book and feel free to contact me at coachdibernardo@gmail.com or at my blog www.coachdibernardo.com

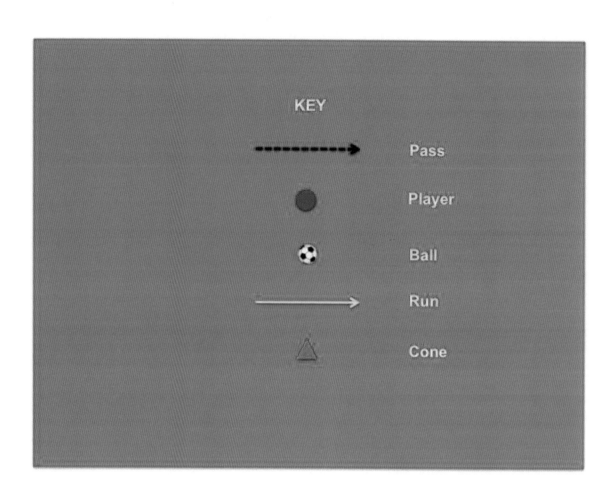

Exercise One
1-Touch Barca Triangles

Grid: 10x10 Yards/4 Grids of 5x5 yards

Instructions: This 1-touch passing pattern requires coordinated movement and rhythm between both groups. The middle players pop out wide after the 2nd pass to form a triangle. Players do not rotate positions. The drill repeats itself after the 5th pass is made. Rotate player positions every 3 minutes.

Key Points: Properly weighted one-touch pass, passing to the receiving player's correct foot, eyes up for field vision and coordinated movement and timing between both groups.

1-Touch Barca Triangles:

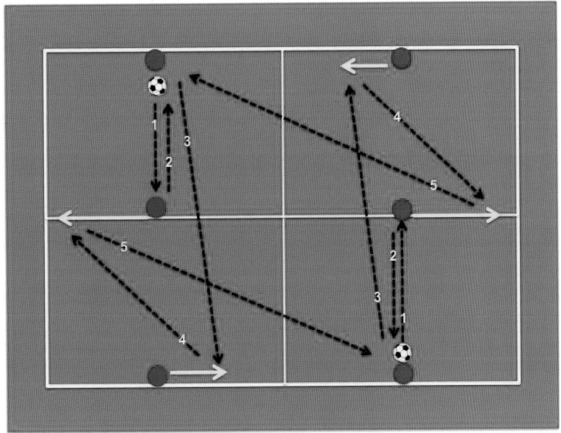

Exercise Two
1-Touch Penetrating Ball

Grid: 15x15 Yards

Instructions: The red players on the outside must make 2 passes before playing the 3rd pass through the cones into a blue player. The receiving blue player must play the ball back to the other blue player through the cones 1-touch, the receiving blue player will then play 1-touch to any red player on the outside. Blue players must stay on opposite sides of the middle cones in order to combine together. The entire exercise is played 1-touch.

s **Key Points:** Properly weighted one-touch pass, passing to the receiving players correct foot, eyes up to see the penetrating ball, blue players must open up to allow penetrating passing coming in and support for the combination, red players should be active on the outside getting into good supporting and passing positions.

1-Touch Penetrating Ball:

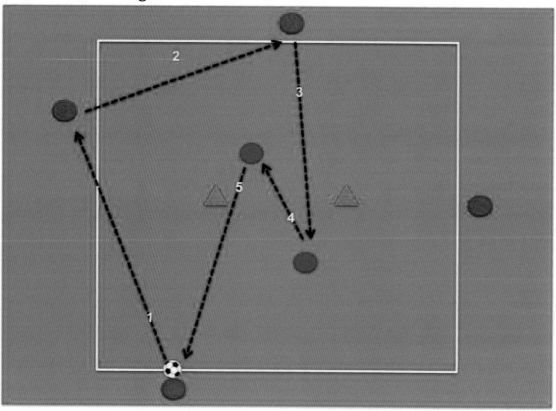

Exercise Three
1-Touch Overlap

Grid: 10x15 Yards

Instructions & Key Points: The red players always stay in the middle. The blue passing player will always overlap the red player he/she passed to and then collect the wall pass. The drill is continuous and can be performed all 1-touch.

Key Points: Properly weighted one-touch pass, passing to the receiving players correct foot, eyes up for field vision and movement after the pass.

1-Touch Overlap:

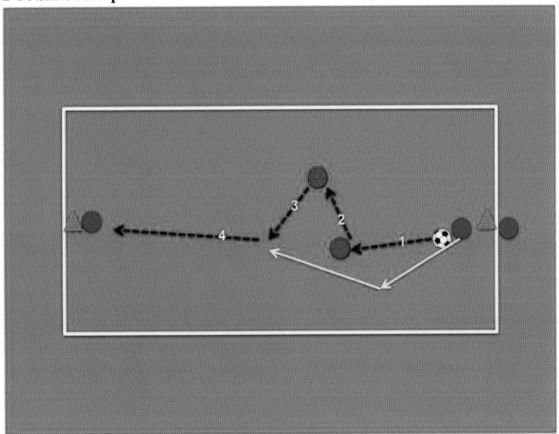

Exercise Four
16 Player Double Diamond 2-Touch

Grid: 15x20 Yards
Instructions: This exercise is mandatory 2-touch. Inside of foot control and inside of foot pass. The passer follows the pass and joins the next line.

 Key Points: Firm 2-touch passing, passing to the receiving players correct foot, eye contact with receiver before passing, be aware of the opposite groups passing and running players.

Double Diamond 2-Touch:

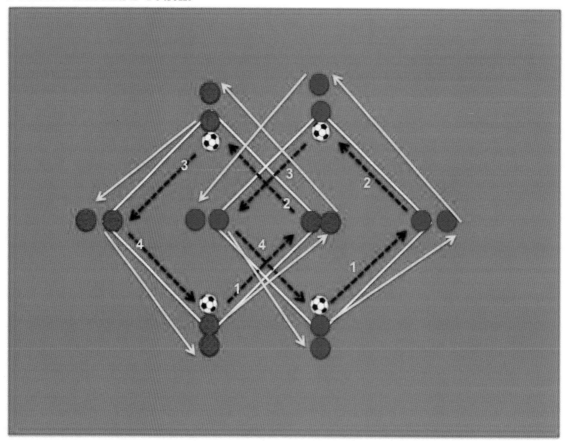

Exercise Five
10 Player 1-Touch

Grid: 20x15 Yards

Instructions: Every pass must be 1-touch. The blue middle players must play quickly. Blue players can start towards middle for the first groups pass and then drop deeper to allow more time for next pass coming from other side. The middle blue players always stay in the middle.

Key Points: Properly weighted one-touch pass, passing to the receiving player's correct foot, eyes up for field vision and proper timing of runs to receive the ball. Timing of the runs and weight of the passes are key to the success and rhythm of this exercise.

10 Player 1-Touch:

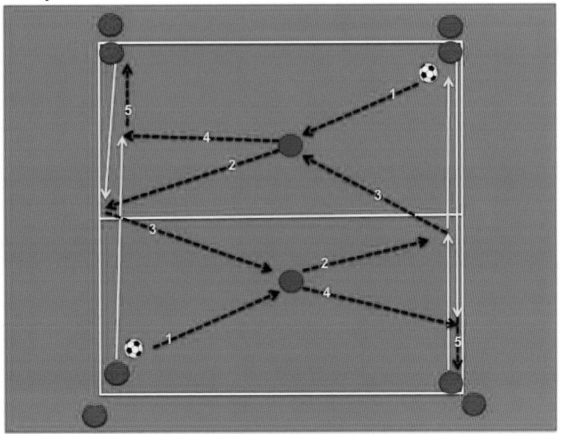

Exercise Six
Circle 1-Touch

Grid: 15x15 Circle Grid

Instructions: The outside player passes ball to the middle player and follows his pass to become the new middle player. The middle player can 1-touch the ball to any outside player, then take up a position on the outside of the circle (close to where he passed)

Key Points: Properly weighted one-touch pass, eye contact with the receiver before passing.

Circle 1-Touch:

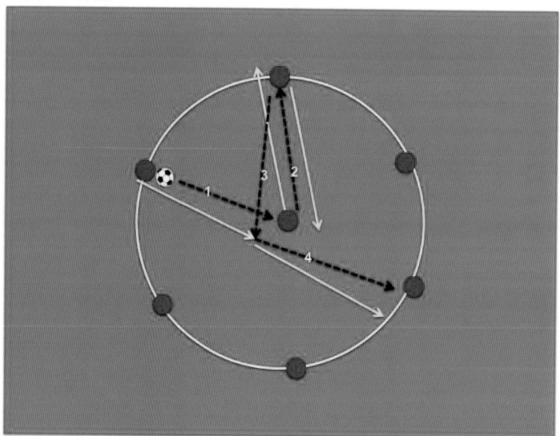

Exercise Seven
8 Player Double Diamond

Grid: 10x15 Yards
Instructions: 2-touch only. Inside of the foot control and inside of the foot pass. Players must keep the rhythm between the 2 balls.

 Key Points: Pass to the receiving player's correct foot, eye contact with the receiver before passing, inside of foot control and pass.

8 Player Double Diamond:

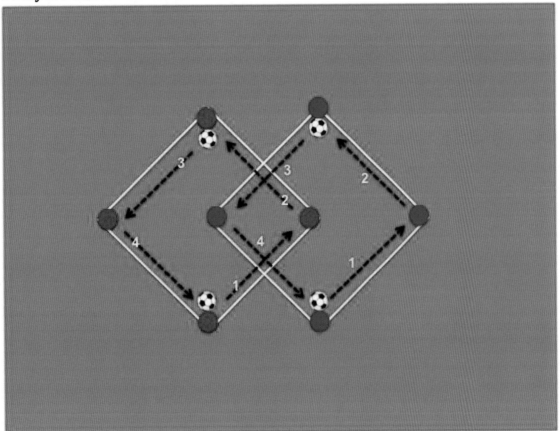

Exercise Eight
5 Ball 1-Touch Tiki-Taka

Grid: 30x40 Yards

Instructions: Every touch must be 1-touch. Players can play in any direction to teammates. Players are free to switch zones with their teammates at any time (players face whatever direction is needed for support). Players can switch the ball to the other side as well, but they can't follow their pass to the other side (example: red player can't go into blue players zones). A high tempo 1-touch rhythm with 5 balls and 16 field players is the objective. Players are looking to form triangles and diamonds to support tiki taka 1-touch passing.

Key Points: Properly weighted one-touch pass, passing to the receiving players correct foot, eyes up for field vision and movement after the pass if needed, effective communication and coordinated movement.

5 Ball 1-Touch Tiki-Taka:

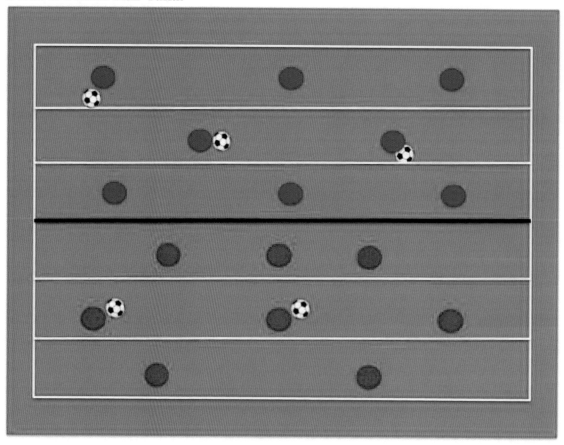

Exercise Nine
1-Touch Diagonals

Grid: 25x20 Yards

Instructions: This drill is to be done 1-touch. The rotation is simply to follow your pass. The only exception is first player who will rotate to the second cone after making pass #3.

Key Points: Properly weighted one-touch passing, passing to the receiving player's correct foot, eyes up for field vision and properly timed movement after the pass.

1-Touch Diagonals:

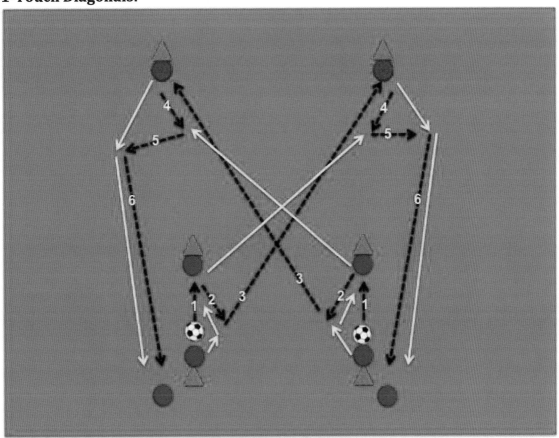

Exercise Ten
Attacking Passing I

Grid: 1/3 of the field (attacking 1/3 – can make it smaller)
Instructions: This passing pattern is in the form of a real attacking movement. After the red team finishes the blue team starts. The red team will recover to their starting positions, ready to go as soon as the blue team passes the ball into the red team's server (in black)

Key Points: Firm passing, passing to the receiving player's correct foot, eye contact with receiving player, well timed coordinated movements.

Attacking Passing I

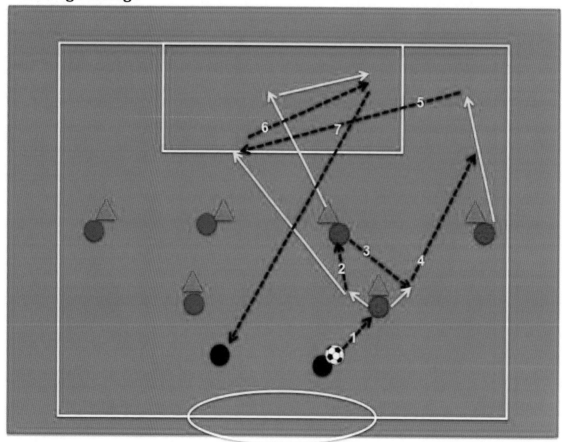

Exercise Eleven
Attacking Passing II

Grid: 1/3 of the field (attacking 1/3 – can be smaller)
Instructions: The two grids are now working together. The recovery of players must be fast because some players are involved in every rotation.

Key Points: Firm passing, passing to the receiving player's correct foot, eye contact with receiving player and well-timed coordinated movement.

Attacking Passing II:

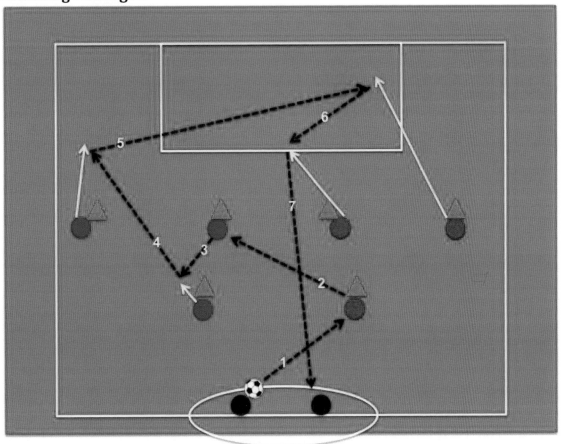

Exercise Twelve
1-Touch Matrix

Grid: 20x25 yards

Instructions: This 1-touch passing exercise must be carried out with rhythm and coordination between groups. Players follow their passes and take up the next position. The only exception is the players on the 3rd and 4th pass (blue and red). The blue player runs towards the corner to make the 7th pass and the red player takes up the blue players spot.

Key Points: Properly weighted one-touch pass, passing to the receiving player's correct foot, eye contact with receiving player, coordinated movement.

1-Touch Matrix:

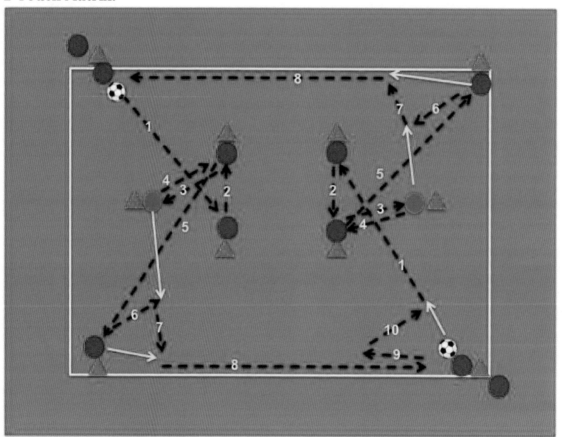

Exercise Thirteen
Positional Team Pattern

Grid: ½ Field

Instructions: The red cones are the starting position for each player. The corresponding white cones are the ending position for each player. The exercise is a combination of 1-touch and 2-touch passing. Moving the ball along the back line is 2-touch, while midfield play is 1-touch. Once the pattern is completed players can rotate forward one position (if you do not want players to rotate – simply do not add extra players and do not rotate)

Key Points: Properly weighted 1 or 2 touch passing, passing to the receiving player's correct foot, eye contact with receiving player, coordinated movement.

Positional Team Pattern:

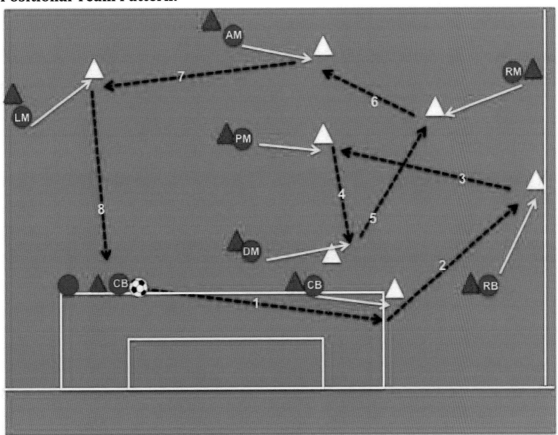

Exercise Fourteen
Partner 1-Touch

Grid: 10x12 yards

Instructions: The blue players start by playing the first 4 passes, after pass #1 & #2 the red players will be in the blue players' positions. The after the 4th pass by blue, the red players will make the next 4 passes. The rhythm is 4 passes for blue and then 4 passes for red. Both groups will be moving at the same time, no matter which group is making the 4 passes

Key Points: Properly weighted one-touch passing, passing to the receiving player's correct foot, eye contact with receiving player, well timed coordination of movement with partner and entire group.

Partner 1-Touch:

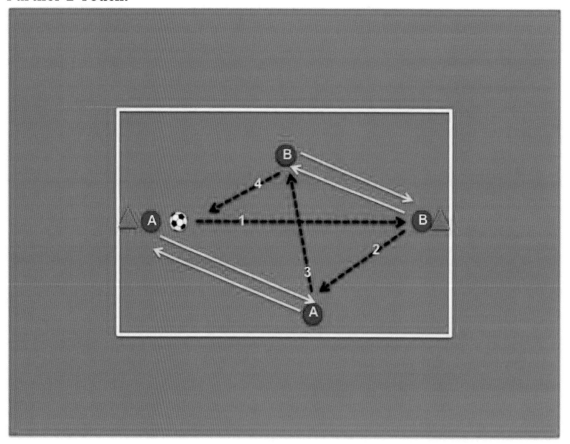

After 4 passes this will be the new starting position.

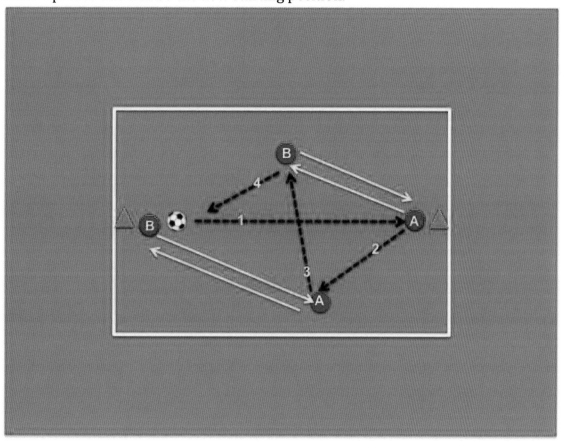

Exercise Fifteen
1-Touch Overlap Wall Passing

Grid: 10x15 Yards

Instructions: The red "A" plays into blue player and overlaps red "B", red "B" takes red "A'" position. Red "A" receives pass back from blue and plays forward into red "C", red "C" plays wall pass with blue and overlaps red "A", red "A" takes red "C" position. The drill continues in that same pattern. The Entire drill can be done 1-touch.

Key Points: Properly weighted one-touch pass, passing to the receiving player's correct foot, eyes up for field vision and movement after the pass.

1-Touch Overlap Wall Passing:

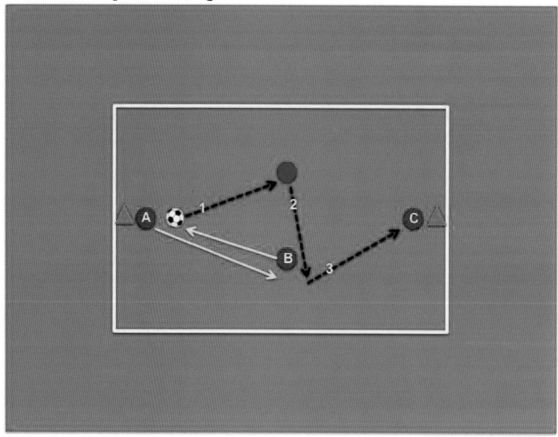

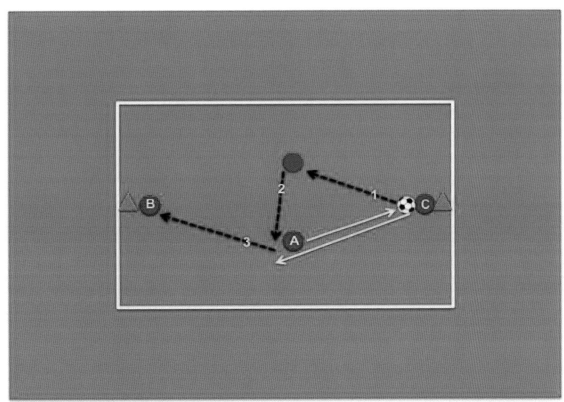

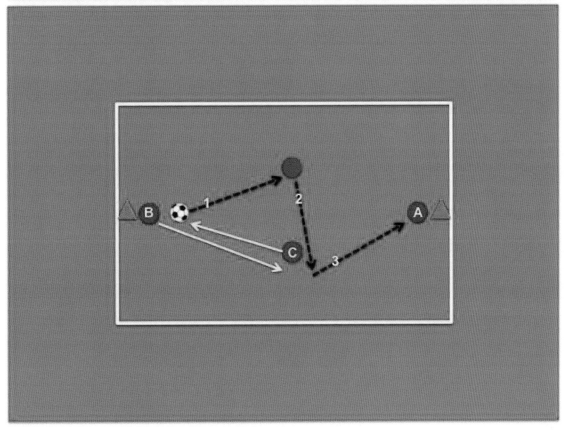

Exercise Sixteen
2 Ball 1-Touch

Grid: 15x15 Yards

Instructions: The red player starts with a 1-2 wall pass with the black player in the middle. The black middle player always stays in the middle as a 1-touch wall passer. The player who does the wall pass (in this case the red player) must make the next pass straight (in this case into the blue player). The player receiving the straight pass will always play a 1-2 with the middle black player. The entire drill is 1-touch and must be coordinated and have a steady tempo. Just remember after every 1-2 is a straight pass & after every straight pass is a 1-2 with the middle player.

Key Points: Properly weighted one-touch passing, passing to the receiving player's correct foot, eyes up, coordinated movement, creating good passing angles.

2 Ball -Touch:

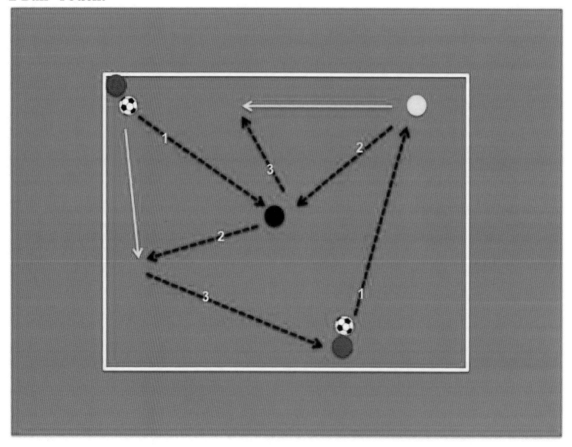

Exercise Seventeen
Double Diamond 1-Touch

Grid: 12x12 Yards – 2 Grids

Instructions: The ball is passed in the sequence as diagramed. However, the red "A" player only switches with red "B" and blue "A" only switches with blue "B" only. As soon as the pass is made players will switch inside their diamond with the same color teammate only. Keep the play 1-touch (2-touch may be required for the 4th pass only if the timing between groups is off). Coordination and tempo of passing between both diamonds is important. A rhythm must be developed so the exercise can be continuous.

Key Points: Properly weighted one-touch pass, passing to the receiving player's correct foot, eye contact with receiving player and movement after the pass.

Double Diamond 1-Touch:

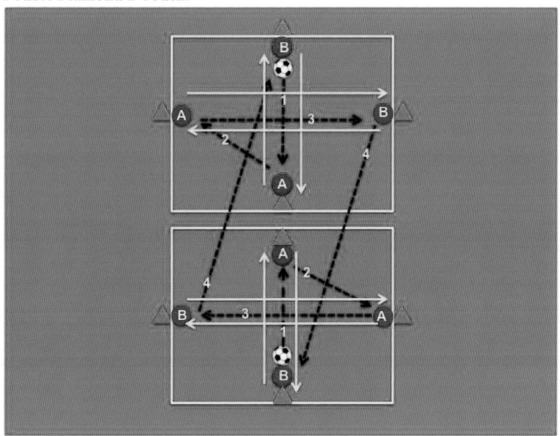

Exercise Eighteen
1-Touch 3 Player

Grid: 10x10 Yards

Instructions: This pattern is carried out with a 1-2 wall pass around the center cone, then a pass back. The pattern is continuous and can be done all 1-touch.

Key Points: Properly weighted one-touch pass, passing to the receiving player's correct foot, eyes up for field vision and movement after the pass.

1-Touch 3 Player:

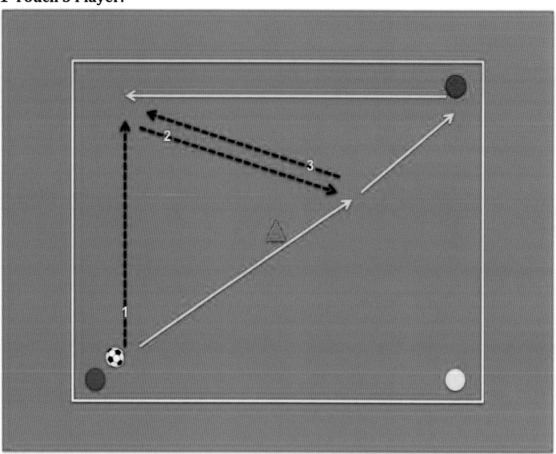

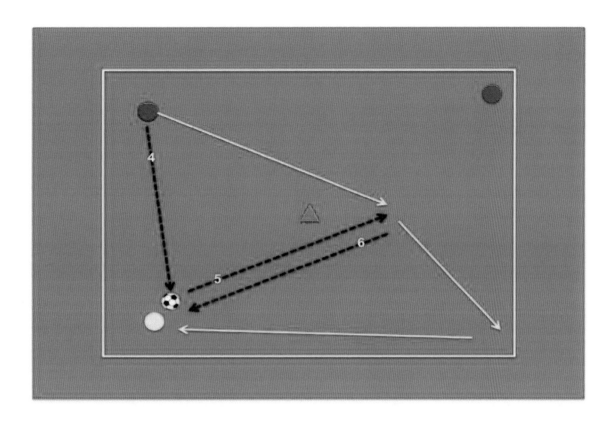

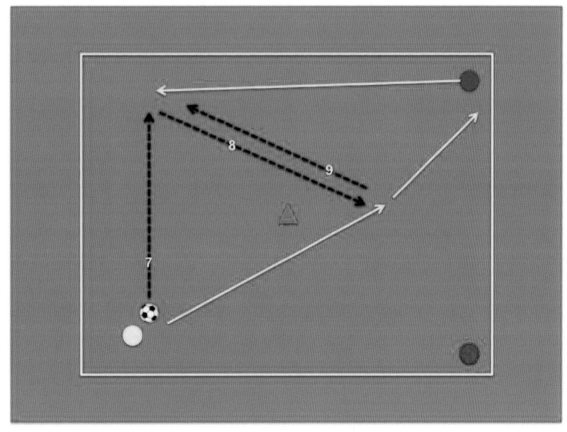

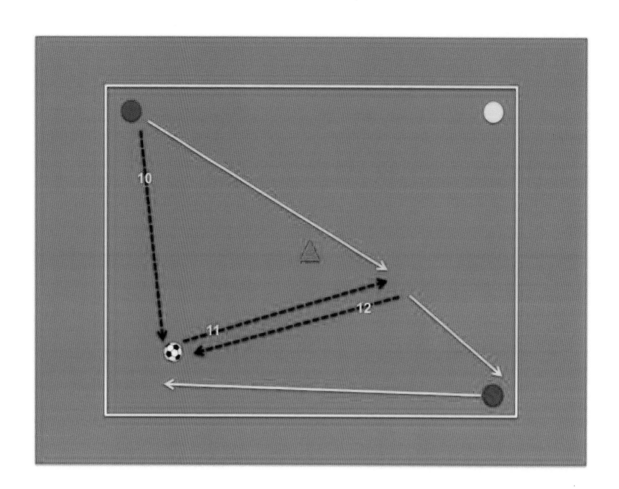

Exercise Nineteen
Diagonal Switch 1-Touch

Grid: 12x12 Yards

Instructions: This 1-touch pattern is done with passing player "A" and "C" moving together. "A" plays into "B" and runs across to receive pass back from "B" as "C" takes the spot "A" left. The pattern continues as "B" and "D" will now perform the same movements as "A" & "C".

Key Points: Properly weighted one-touch pass, passing to the receiving player's correct foot, eyes up for field vision and well-coordinated movement between players.

Diagonal Switch 1-Touch:

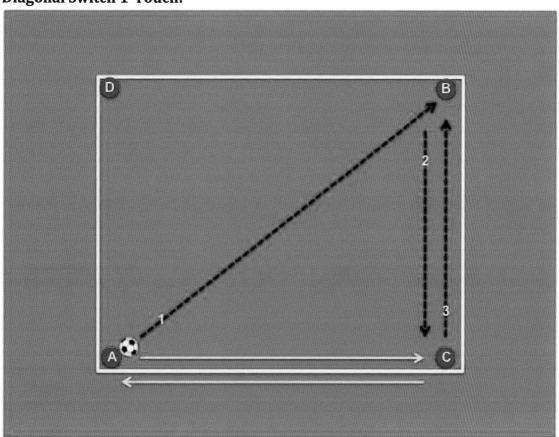

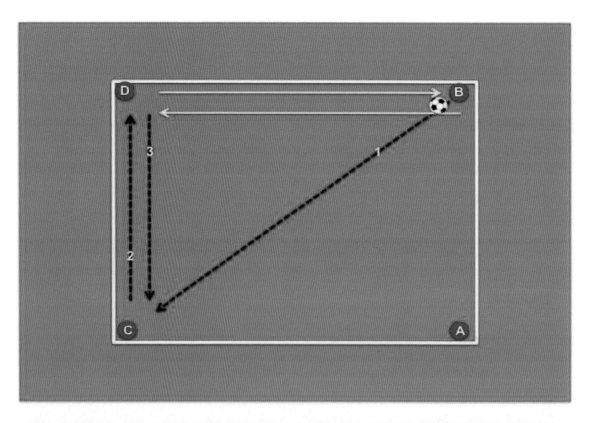

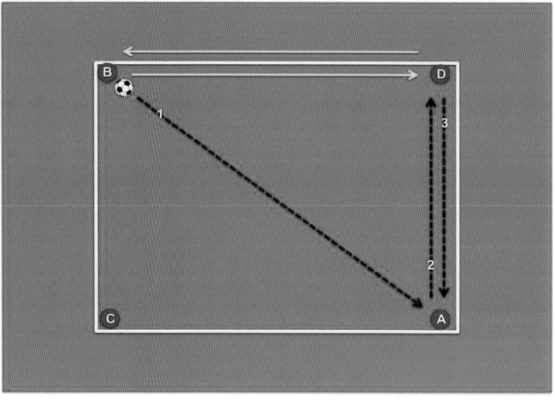

Exercise Twenty
Free Corner 1-Touch

Grid: 10x10 Yards

Instructions: The blue player on the ball plays into the middle red player. The red player stays in the middle and 1-touches the ball to one of the open two blue players. The blue player who passed the ball into the red must run to the open corner. All players play 1-touch. After 2 minutes switch the middle player. The exercise is fast and continuous with a 1-touch rhythm.

Key Points: Properly weighted one-touch pass, passing to the receiving player's correct foot, eyes up for field vision and movement after the pass.

Free Corner 1-Touch:

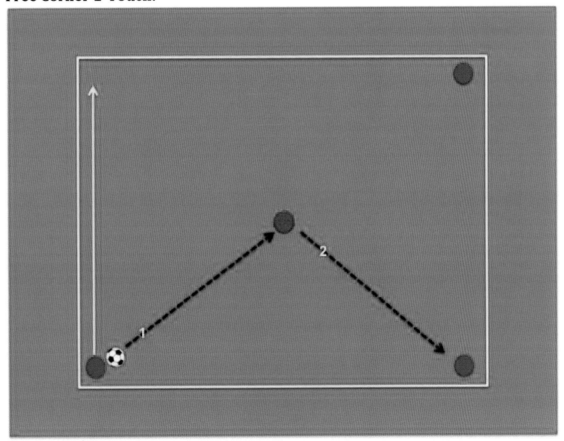

Other books by the author:

The Method - The Art of Coaching & Managing Soccer

The Science of Rondo - Progressions, Variations and Transitions

Speed of thought= Speed of Play

Soccer Smart

Modern Soccer: A Cognitive Soccer Development Model

Problem Solving Skills & Soccer IQ

Cognitive Soccer Passing Patterns & Exercises: Developing Players Technical Ability,

Coaching the Modern-4-2-3-1-Soccer-Formation

45 Professional Soccer Possession Drills: Top Drills From The World's Top Clubs

Professional Soccer Restarts: 15 Corner Kicks that Work

Professional Soccer Restarts: 20 Free Kicks That Work

Professional Soccer Finishing Drills

Professional Soccer Passing Patterns

The Science of Soccer Team Defending

Made in the USA
Lexington, KY
18 March 2015